DANIEL IN THE LIONS' DEN

Louis Weber, C.E.O.
Publications International, Ltd.
7373 North Cicero Avenue
Lincolnwood, Illinois 60646

Manufactured in USA.

8 7 6 5 4 3 2 1

ISBN: 1-56173-722-4

Contributing Writer: Marlene Targ Brill

Consultant: David M. Howard, Jr., Ph.D.

Cover Illustration: Stephen Marchesi

Book Illustrations: Thomas Gianni

David M. Howard, Jr., Ph.D. is an associate professor of Old Testament and Semitic Languages, and is a member of the Society of Biblical Literature and the Institute for Biblical Research.

Publications International, Ltd.

Long ago in the city of Jerusalem, there lived a young boy named Daniel. Jerusalem had been taken over by a king named Nebuchadnezzar. The king said that the people of Jerusalem must follow his laws now.

The king said, "Jerusalem is mine! I order my soldiers to bring all the best royal and noble sons of Jerusalem to my palace in Babylon." King Nebuchadnezzar wanted to train them to work in his court.

Daniel and his three friends were chosen by the soldiers, along with other boys, to come live at the palace in Babylon. This is how Daniel came to live in Babylon.

The king put his palace master in charge of the boys. He was to make sure the boys were well taken care of and taught lessons. The boys studied what pleased the king.

Daniel and his friends learned more than anyone else. God watched over them and gave them wisdom beyond their years. God gave Daniel the special gift of understanding dreams.

Daniel's friends were given special jobs in the kingdom. Daniel stayed in the palace. He became known as someone who had the spirit of God. Daniel explained what no other person could explain. He served King Nebuchadnezzar and every king after him.

Years later, King Belshazzar had a party. During the party, a huge hand appeared and made strange writing on the wall. The king did not understand what it meant. Someone told the king that Daniel might be able to explain it.

The king had Daniel look at the writing. Daniel told him, "You rebelled against the Lord of heaven. You worshiped other gods. You thought they were better than He is." The king thanked Daniel and gave him a very important job in the kingdom.

The next king, named Darius, planned to give Daniel an even more important job. This made some of the other workers angry.

These other men tried to find something to make Daniel look bad. But he had done nothing wrong. They needed a plan. They were going to trick the king!

They went to King Darius and said, "We think that for the next thirty days you should make a law that people can only pray to you. If they pray to anyone else, they will be thrown to the lions."

"That would be nice," thought the king. He signed the paper. He did not realize what the evil men were planning.

Daniel heard about the law. But since he was a faithful servant of the Lord, he continued to pray to God. He would kneel down in front of the open window upstairs and pray.

The evil men saw him praying. They knew their plan had worked. Quickly, they ran back to King Darius. They said, "Didn't you sign a law that said no person should pray to anyone except to you?" "That's correct," answered the king. "Otherwise, they will be thrown in the lions' den."

"Daniel doesn't listen to you," the men reported. "He continues to pray to God. He must be punished as you said."

King Darius could not believe what had happened! He had never meant to hurt Daniel. He tried and tried to find a way to save Daniel. But a law signed by the king could not be changed. There was nothing he could do.

The guards got ready to throw Daniel into the den of lions. King Darius wanted to talk to Daniel. He went to Daniel and said, "May your God, whom you faithfully serve, keep you safe."

The king and his officials put their royal clay stamps on the rock that covered the opening. That way they would know no one had tried to let Daniel out of the den. Sadly, the king went back to his palace.

King Darius was so sad. He could not eat. He could
not sleep. All night long he thought of poor Daniel.
He went outside early the next morning and ran to
the den. "Daniel," he called out, "Are you all right?
Did your God protect you?"

"Yes, king," answered Daniel, "God sent an angel
to shut the mouths of the lions. I have not been
harmed."

The king was so happy! Daniel was okay! God
had saved him!

King Darius could not wait to see Daniel. He just had to see for himself that Daniel was okay. The king ordered his guards to take Daniel out of the lions' den. Many men came to remove the stone from the opening. The royal seal was still there. They lifted Daniel out of the den.

King Darius greeted Daniel warmly. Then he made sure he was unharmed. "I'm so glad you are not harmed," said the king. "Your God protected you."

King Darius went back to his palace. "Guards!" cried out the king. "Bring me the evil men who tricked me and tried to harm my faithful servant Daniel."

One by one, the evil men were brought in front of the king. King Darius was very unhappy with them. He decided that the men should have the same punishment they tricked him into giving Daniel.

Then King Darius wrote to all people throughout his empire: "All the people in my kingdom should obey Daniel's God. This is the God who lives forever. This God saves people. Daniel was saved from the lions."

From that day on, Daniel and his friends lived in peace in the kingdom of King Darius.